INTERNET AND E-MAIL USE AND ABUSE

Clare Hogg, MCIPD, is a consultant and writer specialising in human resources and marketing. As a consultant she covers a wide range of projects – competency frameworks, internal communication strategies, management development programmes – for a wide range of organisations, from major multinationals to small companies, across both the public and private sectors. As a journalist and writer she has written for all the quality press and professional magazines. She is co-author of the MBA-accepted text *Frontiers of Leadership* and currently edits the CIPD Information Notes series. Her other title in this series is *Creating a Staff Handbook* (1999). She is also an accredited company director.

The Chartered Institute of Personnel and Development is the leading publisher of books and reports for personnel and training professionals, students, and all those concerned with the effective management and development of people at work. For details of all our titles, please contact the Publishing Department:
    tel 020-8263 3387
    fax 020-8263 3850
    e-mail publish@cipd.co.uk
The catalogue of all CIPD titles can be viewed on the CIPD website:
    www.cipd.co.uk/publications

INTERNET AND E-MAIL USE AND ABUSE

CLARE HOGG

CHARTERED INSTITUTE OF PERSONNEL AND DEVELOPMENT

© Clare Hogg 2000

First published 2000

All rights reserved. No part of this publication may be reproduced, stored in an information storage and retrieval system, or transmitted in any form or by any means, electronic, mechanical, photocopying, recording or otherwise, without the written permission of the Chartered Institute of Personnel and Development, CIPD House, Camp Road, Wimbledon, London SW19 4UX.

Design and typesetting by
Wyvern 21, Bristol

Printed in Great Britain by the Short Run Press, Exeter

British Library Cataloguing-in-Publication Data
A catalogue record for this book is available
from the British Library

ISBN 0-85292-881-5

The views expressed in this book are the author's own and may not necessarily reflect those of the CIPD.

Chartered Institute of Personnel and Development
CIPD House, Camp Road, London SW19 4UX
Tel: 020-8971 9000 Fax: 020-8263 3333
E-mail: cipd@cipd.co.uk
Website: www.cipd.co.uk
Incorporated by Royal Charter. Registered charity no. 1079797.

Contents

1	Employees, the Internet and the Web	1
2	Employees and e-mail	15
3	How do I recruit using electronic media?	31
4	Internal communication and electronic media	43
5	Training and development resources on the Internet	51
6	How do I create new technology policies?	59

Appendices
A1	Policy content and sample wording	65
A2	Responsibility for equipment and software	79

Resources	81

Dedication

To James, my husband

Disclaimer

The law in this area is changing all the time, and you are advised to seek the advice of a qualified lawyer. Neither the author nor the publisher of this book makes any guarantees or warranties regarding the use of the content of this book.

Other titles in the series

Bullying and Sexual Harassment
Tina Stephens

Creating a Staff Handbook
Clare Hogg

Drugs and Alcohol Policies
Tricia Jackson

Induction
Alan Fowler

Part-Time Workers
Anna Allan and Lucy Daniels

Rewarding Teams
Michael Armstrong

Smoking Policies
Tricia Jackson

Employees, the Internet and the Web

- ☑ Introduction
- ☑ Security
- ☑ Internet access
- ☑ Legal aspects
    Sexual harassment – Copyright laws – More ways than one to skin a cat
- ☑ Your organisation's website
- ☑ Internet policies
    Network security – Accessing the Web – Monitoring – Downloading information - Conclusion

Introduction

Many employees have access to a personal computer, and increasingly with that computer there is automatic access to the Internet and the World Wide Web. Unfortunately, computers are now taken so much for granted that an accompanying explanation of the potential problems – or the considerable benefits – of Internet use is seldom given, with the result that neither employees nor employers are gaining maximum value from the Internet. Even when briefing is given, it is very difficult to get people to listen, because many of them think they already know everything they need to know. You will therefore need a creative approach in order to ensure you have grabbed people's attention.

Explaining the benefits can be covered to a great extent by a media campaign (posters, articles, the in-house magazine, etc) and also through training and briefing. Many employees will ask for help if they feel they are not getting the best out of their computers, especially if they think it will help them short-cut some of the more tedious elements of their jobs. The majority, however, often remain blissfully unaware of the potential problems.

The Internet and the World Wide Web

The Internet and the World Wide Web are two distinct yet interdependent entities.

The Internet

The Internet is an international network of linked computers. It supports a number of protocols that enable the computers to transfer information between one another.

The World Wide Web

One such protocol is HTTP (Hypertext Transfer [*or* Transport] Protocol), the system that allows users to browse the World Wide Web. The Web consists of millions and millions of individual pages, each of which has an address called a URL (Uniform Resource Locator) at which it may be found. Pages are usually linked to other related ones, each discrete collection of pages making up a website.

Security

Good information security management is about organisations understanding the risks and threats they face and the vulnerabilities in their current computer processing facilities. Employers need to introduce common-sense, practical procedures to minimise the risks, and they also need to educate their employees about their own responsibilities. To ensure clarity of understanding of these responsibilities, and to reduce legal liability, employers need a computer information systems policy – and this policy *must* have the commitment of senior management.

The Information Security Breaches Survey 2000 (see page 81) shows that, from a sample of 1,000 organisations, 60 per cent have suffered a security breach over the last two years, but only one in seven has a formal information management security policy in place. Few organisations were able to assess the damage they had suffered as a result of security breaches, but those that were able estimated the cost of a single breach as being in excess of £100,000.

That estimate seems like small beer in the light of the experience of those organisations affected by the 'I love you' bug in May 2000, which cost the world economy an estimated $15 billion. Eighty per cent of the top 1,000 companies in the USA were affected; as the virus spread across Europe a banking network in Belgium was brought down and there was further widespread disruption in Austria, Sweden and Germany. In the UK, the House of Commons was forced to shut down its entire communications system.

The survey commented that 'in the knowledge-based economy, one of the most surprising findings was that 31 per cent of the organisations interviewed maintain that they do not possess any information which they consider to be "critical" to their business or "sensitive" in nature'. But think: if someone from a competitor company walked in and saw hard copies of invoices, that competitor would know prices, margins and much more.

Sensitive, critical information can come in very modest guises.

Internet access

Problems are not limited to security breaches; for the most part they are more widespread, if less sinister. Many organisations are losing a lot of money through uncontrolled Internet access. In a recent employment tribunal case, for example, an employee visited 150 websites within working hours whilst trying to book a holiday! (The case was *Franxhi* v *Focus Management Consultants Ltd* ET 2101862/98, unreported. The tribunal agreed that this was an act of misconduct and that, *because the employee concerned had been given previous warnings* and therefore knew what was considered unacceptable, her dismissal was justified.)

In April 1999 a survey of nearly 200 international companies carried out by Infosec, Netpartners and *Secure Computing Magazine* estimated that a typical large company (1,000 employees) would be losing £2.5 million a year through employees' use of the Internet for non-business purposes – an average annual loss of £2,500 per employee!

Other results of the survey included these statistics:

- 84 per cent of employees were given unlimited access to the Internet

- 76 per cent of workers were using company time to search the Web for new jobs
- 35 per cent of companies did not have a formal policy for controlling Internet use
- 50 per cent of workers were using the Web to visit 'adult' sites.

Legal aspects

The law holds further hazards. Employers are responsible for the activities of their employees when the latter are using the Internet. For example, if software for use in an organisation is obtained illegally, the employer is liable even if it was obtained without his or her knowledge or permission. Employers can help to reduce their liability by showing that they have a policy in place to prevent illegal actions and that appropriate steps (including briefing and training) are taken to enforce this policy. In *Humphries* v *VH Barnett & Co* (London (south) employment tribunal), an employee was put on garden leave after it was discovered that he had been downloading obscene pornography. Further investigation revealed that he had been misusing company time and equipment so flagrantly that he was dismissed without notice. Unfortunately for the employer, the tribunal chairman held that *because there was no company policy* detailing what type of Internet misuse warranted summary dismissal, the tribunal was unable to uphold the dismissal. The nature of the pictures downloaded was so obscene as to amount to gross misconduct, but because the employer had merely put the employee on garden leave for accessing them, the tribunal could not uphold the summary dismissal that was the result of the further misuse of company time and equipment rather than the original downloading incident.

In another case (*Dunn* v *IBM UK Ltd*, ET 2305087/97, unreported), a tribunal found that Dunn had been unfairly dismissed when he was sacked for accessing pornography on the Internet. The tribunal said that there was no clear breach of company policy that could warrant his dismissal. *The individual had not been clearly told that these actions might result in a disciplinary process leading to dismissal.* By contrast, in *Parr* v *Derwentside District Council* (ET 2501507/98, unreported), a tribunal found that Parr had violated his employer's *established* codes of conduct and breached trust and confidence when he downloaded sexually explicit images from the Internet. As such, this was gross misconduct and Parr's dismissal was justified.

Sexual harassment

In another case also involving the downloading of pornography – *Morse* v *Future Reality Ltd*, London (North) employment tribunal Case No 54571/95 – a woman shared an office with several men. Much of her colleagues' time was spent looking at obscene images downloaded from the Internet. Sometimes the pictures were specifically drawn to her attention, such as that of a toy gorilla performing a lewd trick. The woman felt uncomfortable: the men had effectively created a hostile working environment. The tribunal upheld her claim that the pictures, bad language and general atmosphere of obscenity constituted sex discrimination on grounds of harassment. The employer was held liable because no one had taken action to prevent the discrimination.

In case you feel confident that no one in your organisation would engage in this sort of misconduct, it is worth reflecting that the Information Security Breaches Survey 2000 found that 50 per cent of employees surveyed were doing so.

Copyright laws

Much of what appears on the Web is, or claims to be, protected by copyright. The Copyright, Designs and Patents Act 1988 states that only the owner of the copyright is allowed to copy or grant permission to copy the information. Electronic copying of protected material is just as illegal as any other means of copying.

Copyright laws apply not only to documents but also to software. The Federation Against Software Theft (FAST) is making rigorous efforts to counteract the use of illegally copied software. Software should be licensed, whatever the source. Also, copyright law should not be breached when forwarding information.

More ways than one to skin a cat

In one instance an employee began spending four or five hours a day on personal Web-surfing. His colleagues got fed up with doing his work and spoke to their manager. The man was dismissed not for misusing the Internet but for breach of contract: he was simply not doing the job he was contracted to do.

Your organisation's website

Your organisation's website is a wonderful means of communicating your culture, values and mission, as well as much more detailed and useful information. Initial decisions regarding the website – who has responsibility for it, what it will look like and what it will contain – are strategic and should involve the board of directors and certainly the chief executive. There should be clear guidelines regarding who is authorised to put information on the website and how inputs (enquiries, orders, etc) are to be received and handled. If there are images of employees on your website, make sure the employees' consent to have them displayed has been obtained first.

Most organisations like to stipulate who has the ability to post information onto the website or to correct or amend current information. One approach is to make it the responsibility of departmental, section or divisional managers to check regularly that the material relevant to their area published on the website is suitable and is produced by someone who supplies informed and accurate information.

Internet policies

The purpose of an Internet policy is to ensure that:

- employees and the employer get the best out of the Internet
- users are alerted to the commercial and technical risks to the organisation
- everyone is informed of the consequences of misuse – ie that (specified) disciplinary action will be taken.

Before an Internet policy can be drafted, the organisation needs to develop an agreed strategy for Internet use, which should include the degree of network security to be imposed.

Network security

The risk from the Internet to an individual computer is limited. However, most organisations with access to the Internet also have their computers linked to one another through a local network of their own. In this situation the whole network becomes vulnerable either to unintentional or deliberate misuse.

One of the most common and serious sources of damage is the introduction of a virus, which can occur when downloading software or other files from the Internet. Such a virus can spread quickly from one computer to the whole network, damaging software and hardware alike.

Technical security features are available, which can help to protect a network against abuse. These features include the following.

- *Firewalls* provide software protection against unauthorised access. They work by barring attempted access from non-allowed addresses and are generally managed by the IT department. Some organisations block access to sites that are offensive in a sexual, racial or religious manner, or that offer online gambling. However, it is also possible to block access to recruitment agencies, which, considering some of the statistics quoted above, may be a sensible thing to do.
- *Two-factor authentication systems* rely on tokens or 'smart cards' to authenticate users accessing a website and enable an organisation to secure selected pages or sections. SecurID is an example of such an authentication system.
- *Encryption* of sensitive information may be

employed through the use of a protocol. This has to be configured on the server (rather than the user) side. Note, though, that non-escrowed encryption (ie one not kept by a third party) can pose issues concerning the ability of the company to get access to a company record in the absence of the employee who knows the key.
- *Passwords* provide some security at user level. Your policy should clearly state the rules for changing and not disclosing passwords. One of the easiest ways for hackers to find their way into a system is simply to ask an unsuspecting employee for his or her password! The policy should also make it clear to computer users that they are responsible for the security of their terminal, and that they should not allow it to be used by an unauthorised person. Bear in mind, however, cracking a password is not difficult: they can be guessed, stolen or observed.
- *Anti-virus* software provides an element of protection against the importation of viruses.

Accessing the Web

Your Internet policy should state:

- *who* will be allowed access to the Internet (which will generally be via the World Wide Web)
- *how* they will get this access
- *what* use it will be for – business only or private as well.

As for whether employees should be allowed to use the Web for private use, the normal approach is one of balance; this is especially the case where employees work long and irregular hours. Employees do have a need, on occasion, to attend to personal matters during working hours – the point here is however that they should not abuse the system while doing so. It is easier to enforce a 'business only' policy in organisations where people share e-mail addresses; where they work regular hours; or, in smaller companies, where the monitoring task is more feasible.

The policy should also warn users that, although one of the main benefits of the Internet is the vast amount of up-to-date information it contains, it is also entirely uncontrolled and unregulated. The information is not necessarily reliable or accurate.

Monitoring

There is a strong tendency for browsing to become a very unfocused and time-consuming activity, even when carried out for business use. Once involved in a search, people find it is all too tempting to jump down fascinating-looking rabbit holes. This is a waste of the employees' time, and even if it is done in their own time, it ties up the employer's resources and can be expensive in terms of telephone charges (although the use of dial-up lines is now uncommon, especially in larger organisations).

Some organisations monitor the use of the Internet to find out which websites are being accessed regularly and by whom. Most investigations are prompted by line managers, although the IT function of an organisation with a firewall will become aware of individuals who attempt to access inappropriate sites. If employees are monitored, then this should be clearly stated in the policy, together with the action that will be taken against anyone misusing the Internet.

At the time of writing, organisations are in a cleft stick with regard to monitoring. On the one hand, in order to ensure policies are adhered to, and in order to demonstrate a genuine attempt to prevent the development of 'hostile workplaces', monitoring is essential. On the other hand, employers must take account of the Data Protection Act 1998, which came into effect in March 2000, and the Human Rights Act 1998, effective as of October 2000, which incorporates into domestic law the rights of individuals to privacy in their family life, home and correspondence. (It should be noted, however, that many employers will not have to comply with all of the provisions of the Data Protection Act until 24 October 2001.)

In *Alison Halford* v *UK*, Miss Halford's office phone was tapped. The European Court of Human Rights found this to be a breach of the convention, which provides that 'everyone has the right to respect for his private and family life, his home and his correspondence'. The key factor here was the fact that the employee was not advised that her telephone was being tapped. With regard to the Data Protection Act, a code of practice has been drafted by the Personnel Policy Research Unit (an independent consultancy) and approved by the Data Protection Registrar. Employers should contact them to get the latest advice (see Resources on page 82).

Downloading information

There are a number of dangers involved in downloading information from the Internet; the most important are outlined opposite.

- *Downloading offensive, obscene or indecent material.* System managers can bar access to certain sites, but because the Internet is growing so rapidly it is impossible automatically to prevent access to every inappropriate site. Your policy should state unequivocally that downloading offensive, obscene or indecent material is forbidden. It would be difficult to dismiss an employee for using the Internet for inappropriate purposes unless one of your policies (either the computer use policy, or the disciplinary policy, or both) clearly states that this constitutes gross misconduct. However, if the material being downloaded or circulated were regarded as obscene, then the employee might be committing a criminal offence, which could reasonably be considered a matter of gross misconduct.
- *Breaking copyright laws.* Most corporate libraries have a strict policy regarding photocopying, and similar rules regarding copying from the Internet (both documents and software) should be incorporated into your Internet policy. Downloading screen savers has emerged as a particular problem: quite a few are copyright, and they may also have a virus attached.
- *Introduction of viruses.* The greatest risk from viruses lies in downloaded programs and executable files. Spreading viruses is also subject to prosecution under the Computer Misuse Act 1990. You may wish to include in your policy a rule that all software for use in an organisation should be obtained from controlled legal sources by the

system manager. Any other restrictions should obviously also be clearly stated.
- *Time-wasting.* As with browsing, downloading information or software can take a very long time. You may consider including in your policy guidelines regarding what is acceptable in terms of time spent downloading material from the Internet.
- *Material taking up too much room on the system.* Many organisations include a section in their policy on deleting or archiving information – how people should store all the data they download.

Conclusion

Having a policy makes it clear that an employer has done everything possible to ensure that employees are complying with the law. A checklist of items to be included in a computer systems information policy, together with sample wording for a policy, are included at the back of the book. The computer systems information policy includes policies on the use of e-mail as well as the use of the Internet.

An Extranet

An Extranet is an external network for communication between organisations. Many of the issues in Internet policies are equally applicable to Extranets.

It seems likely that, in the future, four or five organisations may join together and pool support functions (such as HR, finance etc). Use of these functions will become feasible through the use of an Extranet.

Employees and e-mail

- ✔ Training
- ✔ Legal aspects
  Employers' liability – Disclaimers – Information that should legally appear on business letters
- ✔ Ensuring the system is not overburdened
- ✔ Using e-mail to bully
- ✔ Monitoring e-mail
- ✔ E-mail policies
  Access – Use – Content – Record-keeping – Wrong delivery – Monitoring – Confidentiality – Etiquette

E-mail has become one of the top ten stresses of working life. A survey of 800 managers carried out by the Institute of Management (see page 81) showed that nearly a quarter of managers said that coping with their e-mail had caused them stress over the previous year, and indeed more so than through having a bad relationship with the boss or dealing with customer complaints.

E-mail:	
Advantages	**Disadvantages**
Fast way of sending messages over both short and long distances	Information overload leads to stress
Cheap way of sending messages	Information overload leads to overlooking of vital information
Information can be shared consistently between any number of people	People using the system unnecessarily or attaching over-large files stretch the computer system
Contributes to the *paperless office* – reduces the need to print and distribute by conventional means	Messages are quickly and easily written and sent – but sometimes the sender does not give enough thought to the implications
Asynchronous messaging allows reflection and research before a message is sent.	It can stifle face-to-face communication, or provide an easy means of communicating difficult or awkward information that should really be given in person
	According to research carried out by Ronin Research, 94 per cent of a sample of over 1,000 respondents said they wasted up to an hour each day reading, responding to or deleting irrelevant messages. Others said even more time was wasted. (See page 82.)

Training

The Institute of Management study shows that high levels of stress arise from new technology foisted, with little training, upon people by IT professionals. Part of the stress is caused by the common perception that e-mail needs to be acted upon instantly. Profligate and thoughtless use of e-mail puts strain on the system itself as well.

The regular sending of more than 2 million e-mails a week threatened to overload British Airways' networks and its people. To deal with this, British Airways launched *The Daily E-mail*, a paper-based newsletter with such headlines as 'Thousands Feared Buried in E-Quake'. The clever headlines grabbed people's attention, and humour was also used to keep employees reading. The newsletter included hints for the use of e-mail, such as those in the box below.

Hints on dealing with e-mails

✔ Unless you are expecting an urgent message, turn off the systems that alert you instantly to the arrival of a new message.

✔ Check your e-mail no more than three times a day – in the morning, the afternoon, and before you go home.

✔ Don't feel obliged to give a detailed, comprehensive reply or to take action immediately. It is usually acceptable simply to acknowledge receipt and explain that you will give a full reply or take action shortly.

✔ If you are replying to an e-mail circulated to many other people, don't automatically reply to the entire original circulation.

> ✔ Make it clear what action you expect as a result of your e-mail.
> ✔ Don't forget the telephone! If you don't know how to respond to an e-mail, speak to the sender for clarification.
> ✔ Don't send an e-mail when you feel angry or critical and, if you receive an unpleasant e-mail, don't reply by e-mail.

In addition a short video satirised some common e-mail habits that can overburden the system, such as leaving overflowing in-boxes or sending large file attachments. The video was used in a touring exhibition that included a series of rolling presentations and a PC clinic with five-minute 'ability boosters'. Questionnaires before and after enabled British Airways to measure the success of the campaign.

Legal aspects

Using e-mail often seems as quick, informal and easy (sometimes easier) as using the telephone, and therein lies the danger. E-mail systems may:

- infringe copyright
- perpetrate fraud
- distribute defamatory statements
- inflict harm on third parties.

Because of the scope of this new medium, the harm caused by a wrongful message may occur more rapidly, or be greater in scope even than that caused by paper documents. When an e-mail is sent, four copies immediately exist: one on the sender's PC, one on the sender's server, one on the receiver's server and one on the receiver's PC. Then there is a good chance that the recipient will copy the message to others. Copies on either servers or PCs will be saved every time the computer system makes a back-up. Once a message has been sent, it is virtually impossible to ensure that no copies survive. It also has the same permanence as any other written form of communication, and as such needs to be subject to the same care and control as other documents.

Remember that e-mail is, in legal terms, a 'discoverable' document, ie one that you may be required to produce in the course of legal proceedings. Deleted e-mail may be held on the system for a considerable time or may be accessible through back-ups. In the Oliver North case, for example, investigators recovered e-mail from back-up tapes that North had tried to erase. The use of company e-mail systems from remote locations may create records of company activities that are not stored on equipment owned by the company.

Employers' liability

Information within an organisation's e-mail can also give rise to legal action. Employers are responsible if employees send e-mail messages that are defamatory or that breach confidentiality or contract. Any such messages will be disclosable for the purposes of legal action.

In the case of *Norwich Union* v *Western Provident Association*, for example, it was shown that untrue and damaging statements about alleged financial problems at Western Provident were circulating on Norwich Union's internal e-mail. This resulted in Norwich Union's paying £450,000 in an out-of-court settlement. In an earlier case, a policeman received 'substantial' damages in an out-of-court settlement with Asda when Asda staff posted an internal e-mail alleging that he was involved in refund fraud.

Below are some examples of employee abuses of e-mail for which the employer may be liable:

- stealing intellectual property – using e-mail to send or receive pirated software
- disseminating pornographic material
- publishing defamatory statements
- sending e-mail containing negligent misstatements or binding the employer in other ways, for example through the inadvertent formation of contracts (in *Hall* v *Cognos Ltd*, Hull employment tribunal, 17.2.98, Case No. 1803325/97 an employee successfully held his employers to a variation of his employment contract allowing late claims for expenses after this had been agreed to by a manager via e-mail)
- using e-mail to conduct sexual harassment of other employees (under the Sex Discrimination Act (S41) an employer is liable for acts of his employees, whether or not these are done with the employer's knowledge or approval).

As with Internet use, employers can help to reduce their liability by showing that they have a policy in place to prevent illegal actions and that appropriate steps (including briefing and training) are taken to enforce this policy. When defending a claim, the employer has to show that all practicable steps have been taken to prevent employees from committing discriminatory acts. It is possible, for example, to install software that monitors and filters inappropriate and abusive content, company confidential information and even CVs. The employer also has to show that problems are dealt with as they come to the attention of managers and are not conveniently 'shelved'. Managers need to be briefed regarding these responsibilities.

Disclaimers

Some protection against prosecution for transmitting incorrect information can be gained by adding a disclaimer either to all external e-mail or to all e-mail in a particular category (eg sales quotations). The wording of a disclaimer may simply be the same as that currently used on other printed documents and be little more than an 'error or omission' statement or it may be a comprehensive disclaimer drawn up by the organisation's legal department. The policy on disclaimers depends on the expected risks to the organisation and should be derived from the original computer strategy.

Some organisations ask staff to ensure that all e-mails incorporate a confidential disclaimer; almost all stipulate that confidential information should be encrypted, and that work should not be e-mailed to and from home.

Confidential disclaimer

This e-mail contains proprietary information some or all of which may be legally privileged. It is for the intended recipient only. If an addressing or transmission error has misdirected this e-mail, please notify the author by replying to this e-mail. If you are not the intended recipient you must not use, disclose, distribute, copy, print or rely on this e-mail. When addressed to our clients any opinions or advice

INTERNET AND E-MAIL USE AND ABUSE

> contained in this Internet e-mail are subject to the terms and conditions expressed in any of (company name)'s terms of business. Incoming communications will be monitored.
> This e-mail has been swept for computer viruses.

Information that should legally appear on business letters

For companies, the Companies Act requires that a company states on its business letters its full name, registered business number, registered office and place of incorporation. Today, business letters are written as e-mails as often as on paper, and so it would be prudent for e-mails to carry the same business information.

Ensuring the system is not overburdened

Employers can ask staff to use e-mail responsibly and not overburden the network, but it is also a good idea to adapt your system to incorporate limits of one kind or another. For example, some employers ask system users to check their in-boxes regularly and to delete unnecessary files, or not to send unnecessarily large attachments. Others simply limit the size of the in-box. It is also possible to install software that limits the size of files received or sent. This type of software might remove animation files automatically if they are more than three megabytes, and the sender would receive an automatic message informing him or her of the action. The use of 'out-of-office' messages can reduce e-mail build-up and also prevent confidential e-mails' being sent to computers that are unattended for a long time. Some organisations try to prevent confidential or valuable information from leaving the premises by disconnecting floppy disk drives.

Using e-mail to bully

> I have noticed of late that the intensity of emotions inside our competitive company is higher than usual. I am convinced this is because of e-mail. Every fight that goes on seems to start with a misunderstanding over an e-mail.
>
> Michael Eisner, Chairman, Walt Disney

A *flame-mail* is an abusive, aggressive or deliberately anti-social e-mail. The Ronin research referred to earlier showed that over 50 per cent of respondents had received flame-mails in their work environment. Curiously, the research showed that men were by far the more frequent victims of flame-mails, and that nearly one in three men who had received them said that they got 'flamed' on a weekly basis. However, men were also five times more likely than women to send flame-mails.

Unfortunately, flame-mails take hardly any time or thought on the part of the bully, whereas the effect of receiving one can be highly damaging. Although most flame-mails are sent and received by men, women tend to react more seriously to them.

Flame-mails beget more flame-mails, because most recipients react by responding with another one. In addition, one in six of those questioned in the research reported that they, or someone they knew, had been officially reprimanded or disciplined by a manager by means of an e-mail. Often the result of a flame-mail was an irreversible deterioration in a relationship, or even a total breakdown of communication.

> **Typical comments from flame-mail recipients**
> 'Whenever I see an e-mail in my inbox from a certain person, I hesitate to open it. It's always worded in a way that makes my hackles rise. Sometimes I don't open it: just delete it without even reading it.'
> 'Managers never have the time to talk you through a problem or explain what you should be doing differently. They'd rather just blast off a nasty e-mail telling you to pull your socks up.'
> 'Continual abusive e-mails from a person I work with have totally destroyed our working relationship – I've requested not to work with him on future projects.'
> 'People in this company like to hide behind e-mail – they're just cowards.'

Obviously, this type of behaviour is not acceptable. It may however be better to stipulate in the disciplinary policy that it is not acceptable to discipline an employee by e-mail, or to cover the issue of bullying and harassment in a separate policy which covers these aspects. The important point is that it is covered *somewhere*, because the problems with bullying and e-mail are so widespread. Legally the intention of the parties is irrelevant if the behaviour in question 'subjects the individual to a detriment'.

Monitoring e-mail

Considering all the above, in particular the legal liabilities, it is clear that employers have a real need to monitor e-mail. To give a particularly blatant instance, employers of one of New York's best-selling daily papers discovered while rummaging through the e-mail of a departed employee just how much online work time can sometimes be personal: the paper's former art director had evidently been designing – while at work – websites for escort services and collecting payment in kind during three-hour lunch breaks.

Is monitoring legal, though? There is no right to privacy in the UK, so employees cannot at present complain on legal grounds of an invasion of privacy. However, the introduction into the UK of the European Convention on Human Rights may change this.

The problem currently is more one of managing expectations: employees consider their e-mail to be private and, as with a personal phone call, they do not expect their employer to be listening in. This is particularly the case where the use of IDs and passwords creates a further expectation of privacy. The solution is to make it clear in the policy that e-mail is not private and that it will be routinely monitored, and to emphasise in particular the organisation's ownership of the computer systems. In reality, most investigations occur only when prompted by line managers. Employees should additionally be warned that their e-mail messages could be intercepted over the Internet.

The Code of Practice to be published under the Data Protection Act 1998 will introduce tighter control over employee surveillance that involves the collection of data to monitor performance or detect problems – for example, the interception of e-mail. Failure to comply with such controls could lead to enforcement action or a claim for compensation by any individual who has suffered as a result of his or her employer's surveillance activities.

New law may also make monitoring e-mail risky. The Regulation of Investigatory Powers Act 2000 makes it illegal to intercept an employee's telephone conversations or e-mail messages without obtaining the permission of both the sender and the recipient. However, the Government has promised to mitigate the effects with a set of regulations enabling employers to continue some kind of monitoring. The Telecommunications (Lawful Business Practice) (Interception of Communications) Regulations 2000 allow interception of employees' communications without consent in limited circumstances, eg to protect networks against viruses.

The law in this area is constantly changing, and it is advisable to get a lawyer to check your proposed computer systems policy before finally implementing it.

If employees' e-mail has shared-access facilities (in order, for example, for colleagues to monitor e-mail during holidays, sickness, business trips, etc), then the need for monitoring is obviously reduced: employees will not want colleagues to see personal e-mail.

E-mail policies

A policy is needed to raise employees' awareness of the issues involved and to ensure that e-mail is used properly, which means (amongst other things) that its use does not give rise to any liability on the part of the employer.

Access

Unless everyone in your organisation has automatic access to e-mail, your policy should state who is allowed access, and how they can get it. In most organisations denying any particular groups access to this valuable communication tool would be difficult to justify and be against the interests of the organisation. It is also helpful to include a statement making it clear who may or may not be given details of any particular e-mail addresses.

Use

The policy should state whether e-mail is to be used for business purposes only, or whether it may also be used for personal communication. If personal use is allowed, should this be in the employee's own time or can it be during office hours?

Consider how the telephone is currently used. If (whether implicitly or explicitly) the telephone is used for private calls, then you may think it is difficult to forbid a similar use of e-mail. Bear in mind, though, that others can more easily hear excessive use of the phone for personal calls, and the telephone does not include the greater security risks (documents in writing, imported viruses, etc) of e-mail.

If you decide to restrict the organisation's computer facilities to 'business use only' (and quite a number of organisations do) rather than simply stating a restriction, it may seem more helpful also to give advice on how to obtain Internet access at home cheaply.

If the policy allows personal use, you may want to put some limitations or conditions on this use. For example, accepting use outside business hours for job-related education or for the support of community activities can be a very practical way of demonstrating support of these things. Some employers stipulate personal use is allowed for 'urgent or emergency purposes only', whereas others are experimenting with the provision of an Internet café.

Whether specific or more flexible (ie where e-mail use is left up to the common sense of individuals and their managers – the employment relationship being solidly based on trust), the e-mail policy should make it clear that employees should use the system responsibly, and that personal use should not be excessive and must not interfere with job performance.

All employees should be given briefing or training on the use of e-mail (see above); having been given this information, they will then know how to avoid abusing the system. Part of the purpose of computer information systems policies and the explanations that go with them is to limit the scope for excuses – especially the 'But I didn't know' type.

Content

Obviously it is impossible to cover everything, but your policy should state that sending offensive e-mails will not be tolerated. Any employee who sends a message to another person that causes offence should be subject to the normal disciplinary procedures, however the message is sent. E-mail has the advantage of being written, and therefore there will be the evidence to back up the complaint. In a recent case, a Scottish housing association dismissed two employees who were sending each other sexually explicit e-mails. The employees won unfair dismissal claims, but the tribunal found them 30 per cent to blame for losing their jobs because they knew the office e-mail system was not to be used to send messages of that nature.

Employees should also be aware (and therefore it should be clearly stated in the policy) that e-mail is subject to the same laws as any other written document. Inaccurate or defamatory statements written by employees on e-mails could be the source of future legal action. Some protection can be gained by including a disclaimer on some or all external e-mail. Your policy should make it clear which types of e-mail, if any, require a disclaimer.

For companies, business letters should also include information required by the Companies Act (see above).

Some employers stipulate that staff should use 'signature' files which give information about the sender, eg his or her name, job title, department and organisation. It is also very helpful if these include a telephone number.

Record-keeping

You may be concerned to ensure proper record-keeping – for example, requirements concerning the keeping of records for six years under VAT rules. However, unnecessary archiving of e-mails takes up valuable computer space. The policy should include guidelines on the regular deletion of old and actioned e-mail.

Wrong delivery

It is useful to include a procedure to cover wrong delivery. The policy could include a statement saying that wrongly delivered messages should be redirected to the right person, and that, if the e-mail message contains confidential information, the receiver should not use this information or disclose it to anyone else. (See box, pp 21–22.)

Monitoring

An employer may choose to monitor e-mail either manually or automatically. If you do monitor e-mail then your policy should clearly and prominently state that e-mail may be intercepted and read. This activity must, of course, fall within what is allowed by the Data Protection Act 1998.

Confidentiality

Most organisations expect staff to encrypt sensitive or confidential e-mails and also to attach confidential disclaimers (see box, pp 21–22). Some even ask that messages regarding the confidentiality of the information appear intermittently throughout the text. Because of the insecurity of the Internet it is also advisable that work is not e-mailed to and from employees' homes. Confidential e-mails should not be forwarded without the permission of the original sender.

Etiquette

There is quite a lot of uncertainty as to the sort of style that is appropriate to e-mails. Many organisations simply leave it up to the individual, but some employees find guidelines useful. In essence, e-mails should be brief and informal, with a helpful subject heading. E-mail text should not be in capital letters, because this is difficult to read and may be interpreted by some as the written equivalent of shouting.

The sample computer information systems policy at the back of this book gives some suggested wording for some of the above items.

How do I recruit using electronic media?

- ✔ Advantages of electronic media recruiting
- ✔ Advertising on the World Wide Web
    Your own organisation's website – Online recruiting sites – Why do job seekers use recruiting sites? – Online CVs – Processing replies – Two groups of specific interest to recruiters
- ✔ An integrated strategy
    Permutations and combinations
- ✔ Legal aspects
- ✔ The future

Conventional recruitment methods continue to be used successfully, but recruitment using electronic media increasingly offers a competitive advantage. The Internet increases the scope for the organisation to fill a vacant position with a better candidate, and to do so more quickly and cost-effectively. According to the 1999 *Internet Recruiting Intelligence Report* published by Logos (see page 82), 67 per cent of companies are already using the Internet to search for CVs. It is estimated that more than half of employers will be using Internet recruitment advertising by 2001.

There are literally thousands of Internet sites dedicated to job and CV postings, along with a multitude of pre-employment services such as background-checking offered online. By 2002 there will be an estimated 16,350,000 CVs posted onto the Net (according to *Computer Economics*, June 1999).

Advantages of electronic media recruiting

In comparison with other traditional media, electronic media have the benefit of wide-ranging coverage, speed of communication and convenient interfaces to sophisticated processing. There is still some debate about the effectiveness of the use of electronic media in the recruitment of senior people, where there has always been a strong element of personal contact. But Internet advertising enables searches on a global basis.

However, in addition to advertising jobs to casual and unspecified website visitors, individuals are increasingly being targeted specifically through direct e-mail using lists bought or built up in the normal way. This approach captures even those 24 per cent of staff who are not surfing the Web for other jobs, as well as the self-employed.

Use of the Internet in recruitment:	
Advantages	**Disadvantages**
Can shorten recruitment cycle time	It works best as part of an integrated recruitment strategy – many organisations lack the knowledge, skills and structure to develop such a strategy
Can reduce recruiting costs	It is not yet the first choice of most job-seekers
It reaches a wider range of possible applicants, with, arguably, a better quality of response	It has been perceived as geared primarily towards IT jobs
It is dynamic and not constrained by either space or time, thus allowing constant updating	Many recruitment sites are still rather sparse
It gives an organisation a more up-to-date image	
It provides global coverage 24 hours a day	
It is arguably easier to track and measure advertisement effectiveness	

Advertising on the World Wide Web

The most common way of using the Internet for recruitment is via the World Wide Web. This can be achieved by using one or more of the following methods.

- *Your own organisation's website.* Normally this would involve adding a few recruitment pages to an existing organisation site.
- *A media site.* Advertisements placed in the traditional paper-based media (newspapers, specialist journals) will often also appear on the relevant publication's website. Sometimes there is some additional information given about the vacancy or a link to the advertiser's website. Job-seekers can trawl net listings of advertisements appearing in traditional media by going to such sites as www.fish4jobs.co.uk (regional papers) and www.bigbluedog.com (*Evening Standard*).
- *A dedicated recruitment site.* A high-profile site (equivalent to a national newspaper) will be relatively expensive, and so a smaller, more specialist site (equivalent to trade press) may offer a more cost-effective, targeted option, eg www.recruitsource.co.uk, an HR recruitment site produced by *People Management* magazine.
- *Data-mining.* Lots of candidates have CVs online. Recruiters can write a specification and use search tools to track down the best matches.

Your own organisation's website

According to the fourth annual recruitment survey published by the (then) IPD in May 2000, 43 per cent of respondents use their own websites to advertise positions. (The IPD became the CIPD in July 2000.) However, relying on this as the only means of advertising limits the pool of candidates to only those actively interested in your organisation. If you are an organisation that employs vocational-type staff (eg the armed forces, the BBC, NASA and some of the larger, well-branded multinationals) advertising on your own site can work very well if you are seeking to attract young people looking for their first job. Remember, you are *marketing* to these applicants; they will be bright, sophisticated people. It is highly advisable to get some marketing expertise in to help make this part of your site look exciting and attractive to the right people. Recruitment specialists can help, as can your own marketing department.

You will also need technical expertise and the resources to deal with a large number of applications. Make sure that the process of submitting an application is kept short – some take as long as three-quarters of an hour – or you will lose many of your best candidates.

The following are examples of recruitment initiatives on company websites.

- The RAF has developed a very exciting and innovative careers section on its website. Anyone interested in joining the RAF can try a series of 'missions' that are fun to do, and give a good idea of the kind of skills the RAF is looking for. Other parts of the site give a lot of information on what is available, and what it is like to work for the RAF.

- You can try out the site for yourself on www.raf.mod.uk/careers
- The BBC also has a section of their website allocated to finding new talent (see www.bbc.co.uk, and look at the BBC talent section) – presenters, script writers, etc. But there is another section for other job vacancies.
- Asda (www.asda.co.uk) has an offbeat and amusing graduate recruitment site that is very effectively targeted at its audience. Applicants who fail the filter quiz are redirected to Sainsbury's website! The interactive process includes a quiz and a video, but the process of submitting the application is clear and short.

Online recruiting sites

Online recruiting sites offer a range of services:

- your own template within the recruiting site, which can be edited as often as you like
- a description of your organisation
- additional banner advertising on the home pages of the recruitment site, which can direct job-seekers to look at your vacancies
- a database that contains details of your vacancies and that is constantly searched for matches with incoming CVs posted by job-seekers
- a customised graduate selection system which makes the graduate recruitment process simpler.

The main criticism of recruiting sites is that they offer quantity and not quality. As a result, the owners of these sites are offering more effective screening methods, such as online questionnaires and even psychometric tests. The problem with the latter is that they cannot (easily) be timed and, more importantly, you cannot be certain of the identity of the questionnaire completer.

The directory Sourceuk.com, which gives access to every job on the Internet, poses a threat to online websites. The idea is that instead of visiting different websites looking for jobs on each one, the job-seeker has only to go to this one website, which acts as a compendium. It will be interesting to see how this develops.

Why do job-seekers use recruiting sites?

- They can search for jobs that match their own requirements – their particular skills and experience, for example, and their choice of location, industry etc.
- They get an automated daily search of new vacancies against these requirements, and are informed by e-mail when there is a match.
- They get help with producing an automated CV.

In addition, today's job-seekers use the Internet to carry out more general research into careers, industries etc. They can consult online news sources to research market trends and look up media coverage of potential employers.

Online CVs

Whereas applicants following the traditional route are encouraged to send short, written CVs, online CVs are much longer. This is because, in order for them to match up with the employer's criteria, they must include all the possible search words that could be used. Equally, the wording of an online advertisement needs to be precise enough to discourage inappropriate applications but detailed enough for automatic searches to make good matches.

How are the replies processed?

Responses received by e-mail or Internet online forms can be processed in the usual way. However, sometimes more responses than usual are received, in which case it is possible to use specialised software to pre-sort the responses. If it is an Internet-provided recruiting system (ie you are not doing this job with your own software, in-house), then there are additional advantages to not having to support the software, install it etc – but, equally, there is a loss of control.

Software may provide the following features:

- CV management
- applicant-tracking, which should ensure complete privacy for your organisation and give information as to which stage the applicant has reached in the process – first interview, offer pending etc
- CV storage and retrieval, which may include paper- and fax-scanning
- Internet job posting, direct from your organisation to all the main job boards, and to news and user groups
- a very powerful search capability, including automatic highlighting of the areas that meet the job criteria
- reporting and statistics capability – for example, the ability to assess the quality of job applicants

from different sources, job boards, advertising, job fairs etc.

In addition, there may be compatibility problems if candidates send attachments with their e-mails in a format that the receiver cannot read. The solution to this is either to invest in the software that allows the computer to read whatever format arrives or to insist on a specific standard.

Two groups of specific interest to recruiters

Increasing numbers of people are using the Internet to find new jobs, but there are two groups that are of particular interest to recruiters:

- *graduates* – almost all UK graduates have had access to the Internet, if not their own e-mail addresses, while studying. Most will be looking for employment, so it is worth setting up or signing up to a specialist graduate recruitment programme (try www.milkround.co.uk which targets 'top' undergraduates)
- *'passive' job-seekers* – 76 per cent of workers are using company time to search the Web for new jobs. A lot of these workers are simply browsing. This group often provides a pool of good candidates – people who are happy in their work, rather than dissatisfied, are often worth employing. This is one of the most difficult groups to reach through traditional methods. Passive job-seekers rarely read the 'help wanted' sections of newspapers. They want to target their search specifically and identify potential jobs rapidly. The Internet is the perfect medium for these potential recruits.

An integrated strategy

Permutations and combinations

Electronic media do not automatically provide the best solution. For certain target markets, advertising at trade fairs or in the specialist press, advertisements posted in libraries or on college notice boards – even direct mail – can be the most effective approaches.

There are a number of ways to combine the capabilities of traditional and electronic media.

- The press advertisement can include an e-mail address for requesting an application form or more information; the application form or requested information are then sent back by e-mail.
- The press advertisement can include a website address for finding out more about the organisation.
- The job-seeker can send a CV as an e-mail attachment.
- Those processing the response can either view the applications on-screen or circulate them electronically to the relevant department.
- Employers can put vacancies on their own intranets.

Legal aspects

The code of practice under the Data Protection Act 1998 published in July 2000 is intended to introduce tighter control over automated processing (especially CV-scanning), aptitude and psychometric testing, and the extent to which employment decisions may be taken by automatic means. Failure to comply may lead to enforcement action or a claim for compensation from any individual who has suffered as a result of failure to follow the code.

The future

In the USA organisations are extending the electronic recruitment process to conducting assessments such as psychometric or aptitude tests, online. These tests still need to be conducted in supervised groups, but the process significantly reduces the administrative burden of distributing, collecting and marking written test papers.

Several organisations are also looking at the possibility of conducting remote interviews with a video link. However, the limited bandwidth available on the Internet means that the image is still poor quality, and conventional video links are likely to be used for some time to come.

Internal communication and electronic media

- ☑ E-mail and an intranet as complementary media
- ☑ An intranet and the HR function
- ☑ A typical intranet
    Building an intranet – Measuring the success of an intranet
- ☑ Caveat

An intranet is an internal network similar to the Internet but used for communication *within* an organisation. It includes one or more websites. Intranets need to be kept strictly separated in order to avoid serious security implications. The reason for this is that they often contain a goldmine of information for which competitors would give their eye teeth: market research reports, product launches, technical and price data, quoting guidelines and customer lists to name only a few examples. Intranets are cheap and easy to use, and so long as they are protected by corporate firewalls security is less of a concern than it is with the Internet (although, as just stated, it is not to be neglected!).

The organisational intranet is becoming a core factor in

the internal communications strategy. There is still, and always will be, a need for face-to-face group discussions of one kind or another – and the trend does not apply to everyone: there are obvious access issues where some employees have no desktop PC – but the intranet is reducing the need for printed company newsletters and magazines.

Instead of the old traditional 'top-down' approach to employee communication, intranets allow employees to post information themselves, so that organisational communication becomes bottom-up and lateral – altogether more fluid. The person (or department) responsible for communication becomes less of an information provider and more of a gatekeeper.

A recent employee survey at IBM showed that employees find the most useful information is the knowledge-based, intellectual capital of colleagues. The internal communications function now incorporates the facilitation of information-sharing.

Establishing an intranet will not in itself generate a return on investment. That will come only when employees use their intranet as an effective tool in day-to-day business activities; indeed, ensuring that employees do use the intranet is the most challenging part of the whole process. Furthermore, a lot of problems arise when it is not clear who has overall responsibility for the intranet. Because most functions and departments are represented on it, struggle for 'prime sites' can result in bitter turf-wars. A project team can help reduce such squabbles. Additionally, senior management involvement is essential to ensure the system is effectively sold, with all departments included in the process.

Finally, an intranet is not the automatic answer to everything: for example, if your company is factory-based, it may not be appropriate at all.

E-mail and an intranet as complementary media

E-mail and an intranet create a balance for each other. The e-mail system allows an organisation to get information in front of employees, including new information also on the intranet site. An organisation can for instance send an e-mail 'alert' message with a hypertext link that points the employee to supporting materials on the intranet. These messages can be targeted at specific individuals or groups of employees.

Conversely, the intranet system allows employees to take the initiative and search for news and information of specific interest to them. It may be a good idea to send an all-employee e-mail once a week giving the main headlines, a short summary and the URL address for quick skimming. Otherwise global e-mails should be restricted to strategic letters from the chief executive and to emergencies, such as virus notices.

An intranet and the HR function

An intranet has three main functions for HR:

- knowledge management and transfer – document libraries, discussion groups, training and development (see Chapter 5)
- internal communication

- personnel – self-serve and personnel record systems.

The HR department will often have its own website. This is likely to begin with simple static documentation such as employee handbooks or job postings. The next step is to put on 'live' information that can be updated. Eventually, many sites progress to allowing staff to enter information for themselves. If employees are able to report sickness on the intranet there is much more scope for analysing absence trends. Some organisations even allow the intranet to be used to help arbitrate on leave requirements.

What can usefully be included in the HR website of an intranet

- Induction course (including health and safety briefing)
- Internal telephone directory
- Newsletter
- Employee handbook
- Expense claims
- Booking annual leave
- Online training (see Chapter 5)
- Employee attitude surveys
- Quality manual
- Internal vacancies
- Materials and forms regarding the appraisal system
- Training, including the provision of online training
- Competency framework
- Applications for season ticket loans
- Job application forms

There are hurdles – mostly concerning data security – to overcome in allowing employees access to personal data. The problems can be overcome by using a variety of measures, for example allowing employees access through an extra password known only to them; programming PCs accessing the intranet to log off automatically if they are left unattended for 15 minutes; and changing passwords regularly.

A typical intranet

An intranet site includes an organisational home page with links to other specialised (functional, geographic) sites. General and strategic issues are featured on this home page, but for employees key information lies in the links. Under certain circumstances, parts or all of the intranet may be available in translation.

> **How do you know whether your intranet is effective?**
> - Does it improve business efficiency in measurable terms?
> - Can it be accessed by remote or mobile employees?
> - Do your users make suggestions or ask for additional facilities?

Building an intranet

If your intranet is to contribute to improving business efficiency, the best starting-point is to look at some typical jobs and consider what information and tools would help support these activities. Service engineers (with laptops) out visiting customers could for example find customer or technical information useful. The site should be so well designed that the engineers do not have to search arduously for the information they need.

The parcels division of the Post Office has a cost calculator, for example, that allows its operators to take information on parcel weight and location from callers and find the cost of delivery. Because the calculator is on the intranet there has been no need to install it separately on every individual computer. However, if the intranet does provide essential tools to remote users, consider what would happen if the user's PC or the server failed.

In a small company intranet content can be held on a single site composed of a number of different 'pages'. On larger sites this is no longer practical. It is beyond the scope of this book to outline the technical aspects of setting up and running an intranet – although there are some excellent books on this subject (see Resources on page 82). You can buy off-the-shelf intranet software, of which there are many providers.

The most important points are that an intranet should be easy to use and contain the information that people really need. The more the site is structured so that users can easily find the information they need, the better. Search facilities, which often produce many results that take time to sift, should be considered a last resort. People have limited time, so the site needs to be quick to download. (Try accessing the site from a machine that has a very low specification.) Also make sure that the text is easily legible – not too closely packed or in too small a font. The writing style should also be informal and have some pizzazz (see 'Writing for the Web' in Resources, page 81).

> **E-paternalism, the new employee portals**
> There are a number of employee portals, such as perksatwork.com, which set up employee shopping discounts and related personal finance and travel services via off-the-shelf corporate intranets. Transactions are paid for centrally and deducted from payroll.

Measuring the success of an intranet

Success should not be measured simply by the number of hits. It is better to measure it in terms of the help that the site gives. Ask for electronic feedback from users, and monitor the frequency with which different pages are accessed. There is no point in spending a lot of time and effort providing information and keeping it up to date if it is not used.

Caveat

New technology has (ironically) made face-to-face employee meetings more important than ever. Those tempted to rely completely on electronic media would do well to contemplate this fact. In large corporations internal 'tradeshows' have been shown to be both popular and effective. They are similar to industry tradeshows, different divisions or functions having their own stands and employees having a chance to see recent projects developed by colleagues. Most important of all, the internal tradeshow gives employees a chance to chat in person, to build trust and relationships; these contacts can then be continued via electronic media. But annual company meetings, executive roadshows, team meetings and 'walking the talk' are all other important opportunities for face-to-face communication. They should not be neglected, as the intranet sucks resources towards itself – if anything, the emphasis needs to be realigned towards these critical, traditional forms of communication.

Training and development resources on the Internet

- ☑ Training for new technology
- ☑ One-off solutions
- ☑ Piloting Web-based training

At the 1999 launch of KnowledgePool Ltd, Europe's largest IT training provider, the company predicted that within three years anybody who had not embraced online learning risked becoming unemployable. The growing popularity of online learning has led to a proliferation of terms – 'Web-based training', 'interactive distance learning', 'intranet-based training' to name but a few – but technological advances are blurring the edges of these once-separate categories. Even the term 'interactive' is open to interpretation – it could refer to a 'virtual' chat room or simply the posting of questions onto a bulletin board – but the degree of interactivity available is constantly rising (eg synchronous, two-way, audio-video interactivity). The one thing to avoid is simply to replicate the classroom environment in electronic form.

One of the main reasons organisations adopt online learning is that the required data is available whenever learners want to learn. Business units require:

- small chunks of learning
- support for single tasks
- access to knowledge and expertise.

This explains the increase in integrated programmes that blend technology-based learning with classroom-delivered training.

Benefits of computer-based training
- Reduction of travel expenses
- Consistent delivery of training
- Global access
- Learning delivered in 'bite-size' pieces
- Learning delivered at a time and place convenient to the learner
- People can choose their preferred medium

Training for new technology

Not surprisingly, technology often provides the best media for training people to use new technology. Yet, amazingly, this training is often omitted altogether, especially if the purchase was originally IT-led. A Mori survey of 900 workers in 316 firms carried out on behalf of Compaq and One2One showed that half the men and three-quarters of the women in firms of fewer than 500 employees felt they could not cope with new technology. A quarter of the respondents thought that it would be a waste of time and money.

> **University for Industry (Ufi)**
>
> University for Industry is a new public–private partnership which aims to boost the competitiveness of business and the employability of individuals. Working with business and education and training providers it will use modern technologies to make learning available at a time and place to suit the learner – at home, in the workplace and through a national network of learning centres.
>
> 'Learndirect' is the name of Ufi's network of learning centres that are being developed nationwide. For further information, phone 0800 100 900.

One-off solutions

Initially it may make sense to test online training by dealing with requirements on a case-by-case basis. Learning portals on the Web (such as www.click2learn.com) offer a gateway to a wide range of online programmes, books, CDs and other learning materials. Other companies (such as www.learningmatters.com) offer 'just-in-time training' – bite-sized chunks of learning that can be plucked off the Internet in time for that tricky appraisal or sales exhibition. Yet other providers (for example www.netg.com or www.xebec-online.com) give a whole system to companies. The best solution is often a mixture of different services. A mixture offers individual employees the widest range of options: after all, everyone has different needs. Different people learn most effectively in different ways, some preferring to have control over their learning whereas others prefer to be spoon-fed. So long as the employer maintains control over the budget and the quality, then the more closely individuals can match their requirements with the learning on offer, the more effective the training will be.

Piloting Web-based training

If you are aiming to introduce Web-based training across a large site, a pilot program will establish the best way of implementing it and give a good demonstration of how the system could work for your organisation. Implementing Web-based training has high fixed costs and is a complicated computer technology requiring input from a variety of people, so running a pilot is essential. Another reason for doing so is that a commitment to Web-based training requires a considerable investment of both time and money. A formal pilot can give a helpful insight into how well the proposed solution fits the organisation's business requirements and culture.

The flow chart on page 57 gives a broad outline of the stages involved in piloting Web-based training. The first step is to agree the purpose. It may seem obvious, but it is amazing how often it just seems to come down to 'what everyone else is doing', with the focus on the tools and not on the value of the training for the organisation. Ask these questions:

- How would Web-based training do things better than our current arrangements?
- How will employees benefit?

- Is Web-based training technically feasible?
- What are the real benefits and limitations of Web-based training for my organisation?

Defining your purpose clearly will make it easier to gain acceptance and enthusiasm from others, and it will also make it easier to evaluate the training.

The project will need a champion with influence and impressive skills of persuasion and presentation, eg a member of the board. If you can persuade such a person of the enormous benefits and advantages to be gained, he or she can ensure that the resources necessary to run the pilot effectively will be there. Getting the initial acceptance of your champion may require a persuasive business plan. If you cannot identify the people you want for your project team, at least describe the skills you need, and be honest about the likely costs.

Your project team should have time dedicated to the pilot and be accountable for its success. They should also be authorised to:

- assign workers to create user-accounts
- provide subject matter experts
- enlist support from field offices
- purchase software and hardware.

The team has to define the assessment criteria and then assess the pilot outcomes. Whoever spearheads the team should be prepared for the project to become full-time. The team needs to decide evaluation criteria, which could be for example:

- a certain percentage of trainees completing their learning programme

- a certain percentage of line managers reporting improved productivity from Web-trained employees
- course development time being the same as that of traditional courses
- less than a certain percentage of trainees calling the help desk.

Decide which criteria are important, and even consider weighting them.

When planning the roll-out, remember to start early, not to make assumptions, and have back-up plans. Carry out a dry run to ensure you catch spelling errors, bad menu links, and confusing directions. In summarising the experience of the pilot, ask the following questions:

- What does the data reveal? Are there contradictions?
- How did the pilot measure up to the evaluation criteria?
- Did the participants like Web-based training as a delivery method?
- What did they like and what did they not like? Was there anything that surprised them?

Present your report before your data becomes out of date!

Piloting Web-based training

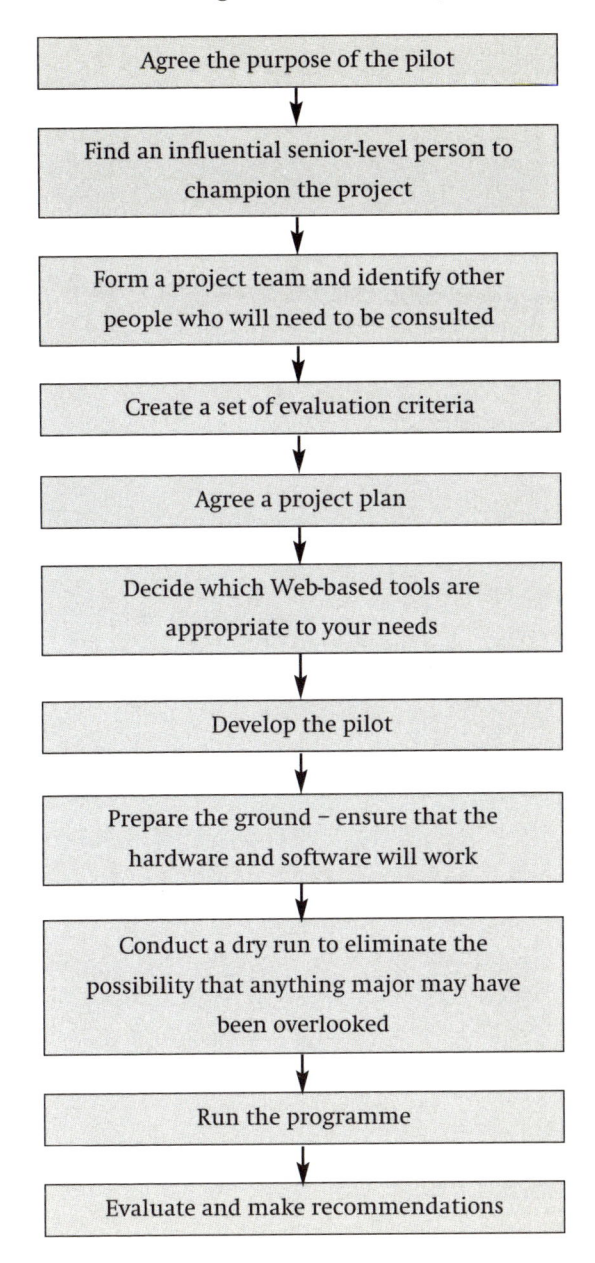

```
┌─────────────────────────────────────────┐
│     Agree the purpose of the pilot      │
└─────────────────────────────────────────┘
                    ↓
┌─────────────────────────────────────────┐
│  Find an influential senior-level person to │
│         champion the project            │
└─────────────────────────────────────────┘
                    ↓
┌─────────────────────────────────────────┐
│  Form a project team and identify other │
│   people who will need to be consulted  │
└─────────────────────────────────────────┘
                    ↓
┌─────────────────────────────────────────┐
│     Create a set of evaluation criteria │
└─────────────────────────────────────────┘
                    ↓
┌─────────────────────────────────────────┐
│          Agree a project plan           │
└─────────────────────────────────────────┘
                    ↓
┌─────────────────────────────────────────┐
│   Decide which Web-based tools are      │
│       appropriate to your needs         │
└─────────────────────────────────────────┘
                    ↓
┌─────────────────────────────────────────┐
│            Develop the pilot            │
└─────────────────────────────────────────┘
                    ↓
┌─────────────────────────────────────────┐
│  Prepare the ground – ensure that the   │
│    hardware and software will work      │
└─────────────────────────────────────────┘
                    ↓
┌─────────────────────────────────────────┐
│  Conduct a dry run to eliminate the     │
│ possibility that anything major may have│
│           been overlooked               │
└─────────────────────────────────────────┘
                    ↓
┌─────────────────────────────────────────┐
│            Run the programme            │
└─────────────────────────────────────────┘
                    ↓
┌─────────────────────────────────────────┐
│    Evaluate and make recommendations    │
└─────────────────────────────────────────┘
```

How do I create new technology policies?

> ☑ Formulating the policy
> ☑ Communicating the policies
>   Types of media – Induction – Training
> ☑ Enforcing the policies
>   Disciplinary action – 'Reasonable' enforcement – Keeping the policies effective

Formulating the policy

Before you begin, find out how computer systems are currently being used in your company. Speak to users, managers and IT specialists. Ask whether employees think their e-mail is private, and how they receive documents from outside. Find out who has access to the Internet. Once you know what people are doing you can identify potential problems or issues to be highlighted. Sometimes your lawyer can supply a draft, which you can adapt, but make sure the policy is comprehensible and does not contain too much 'legalese' or other technical jargon.

Having produced the document, get others to review it and give their comments and opinions. It is also advisable to get your lawyer to check it.

If you are a large company, it will be advisable to form a working party – see the table below.

\multicolumn{4}{c	}{New Technology Policies Working Party}
HR department	Internal communications department	IT and legal department	CEO, board, senior management
Disciplinary procedures	Publishing and communicating the policies	Technical knowledge – especially regarding implementation	Give weight and authority; liaise with/involve board if necessary
Administrative procedures			Ask for a 'reality' check
			Ensure that the policies tie in with business goals and corporate strategy

It is also advisable to consult the relevant trade union(s) or staff association.

Communicating the policies

Communicating the policies is an essential part of the whole exercise. The policies must be understood to be business policies rather than HR or IT issues, and as such they should be championed and signed off by the chief executive. It is important, in particular, to raise the profile of the 'cyberliability' issue, but it is also important to explain why the policy is necessary and what the sanctions for misuse are.

Types of media

The following are media that can be used to communicate the policies:

- hard copy – these policies should accompany the organisation's other employment policies
- intranet
- global e-mails to introduce the policy, and also to remind staff of the policy (especially after an infringement of the rules)
- induction
- follow-up sessions (for example, two months after induction)
- training
- in-house publications
- electronic message that appears on a regular basis (eg every six months) on computer screens to remind employees of the regulations and require an electronic response to confirm the policy has been read and understood
- posters on noticeboards
- roadshows and exhibitions
- team meetings.

There will be far greater understanding and acceptance of the new policies if there is an opportunity to discuss them and ask questions. But if managers are to run briefing sessions they need to have good briefing materials and to be well briefed themselves. It is a helpful technique to use a series of illustrative scenarios, followed by a question and answer session.

Induction

The policies can be outlined during induction prior to giving the new employees their passwords and security codes.

Training

The following is an example of a typical training checklist.

Electronic media training programme
Use of the organisation's e-mail system
Access to and use of the Internet; search methods
'Cyberliability' session, followed by a question and answer session
The organisation's policy on monitoring
Enforcement of the policy

Enforcing the policies

The implementation of these policies is a management issue (rather than an IT or HR responsibility), so line managers are responsible for ensuring that employees comply with the rules and that abuses are dealt with effectively. The role of the HR function, meanwhile, is to:

- advise on policy and procedure
- keep a record of attendance at training sessions

- get all employees to sign a computer usage policy, to show they have read and understood the terms – this is important, because for many organisations the main purpose of the policies is to demonstrate that they have done what they can to prevent misuse. The employer needs to be able to eliminate the 'I didn't know' excuse. If your employees withhold consent, remember that there are exceptions to the need for it, even under data protection legislation.

Disciplinary action

Any disciplinary action taken will be dependent on the seriousness of the abuse. Gross misconduct may include a conscious and deliberate breach of the electronic media policies resulting in damage to the organisation's reputation or in an irreparable breakdown of trust between employee and employer. In other cases consider:

- damage to the computer systems
- reduction in productivity
- breaches of confidentiality and security
- putting the organisation at risk of prosecution
- the creation of an unhappy, aggressive or hostile working environment.

In general, particularly in the case of a first offence, employers tend to deal with transgressions on an informal basis. If formal action is taken, it is good to raise awareness and give credibility to the policy by reporting what has occurred (without necessarily naming individuals).

'Reasonable' enforcement

In policing computer systems policies it is essential to be flexible and reasonable, and not to go 'over the top'. If every transgression is picked up, the policies will become devalued.

Keeping the policies effective

Once introduced, remind employees of the policies' existence at regular intervals. Put in effective auditing processes. Make sure the disciplinary sanctions, where warranted, are effectively applied. Remember, the law may change, and the policy should be regularly updated to ensure it remains compliant.

Appendix 1: Policy content and sample wording

Because many items to be included in an Internet policy can also be applied to an e-mail policy, in order to avoid duplication it is often sensible to combine the two. It is also important to make sure that all your policies are consistent – for example, your disciplinary, anti-harassment and data protection policies should all set out the same rules and penalties.

Your policy should form part of an employee handbook or other document containing employee policies and procedures. As such, it should also be introduced and explained to new employees during their induction and to existing employees in a series of specialist briefing or training sessions.

It is a good idea (and possibly a legal requirement) to consult your works council or trade union regarding the policy. Because liability can be created by those who are not formally employed (self-employed, temporary, subcontracted etc) your policy should apply to everyone with access to your systems.

Not all the items listed below have to be included in a policy, and there is one item you may consider adding: a provision for employees to raise grievances about other people's use of the computer systems.

Most employers will at first try to resolve issues informally, but the policy should form part of each employee's terms and conditions of employment. The disciplinary action to be taken if these regulations are transgressed, and informal warnings ignored should be clearly stated (and upheld). Such action may range from an oral warning for mere lack of consideration to instant dismissal for illegal activity.

The following are the main items to include in the policy, together with sample wording.

General policy statement

It is a good idea to have a box at the top of your policy (highlighted in bold or red type) containing a warning of the importance of complying with the policy and of the monitoring procedures.

The following should also be considered.

- What is the purpose of the policy and why is it necessary?
- Definitions – does this policy, for example, extend to WAP (Wireless Application Protocol) phones?
- To which computers do these policies apply?

Sample wording

IMPORTANT – YOU MUST READ THIS

This document forms part of your contract of employment. By signing the attached document you are agreeing to abide by the terms of this policy. Failure to comply may result in disciplinary action, up to and

APPENDIX 1

including termination of employment, or in the case of non-(*company name*) employed workers, termination of service agreements. In all cases it may lead to civil or criminal liability and/or recovery damages.

The use of the (company name) computer systems is logged and monitored.

These guidelines have been developed and issued in order to enable both (*company name*) and its employees to use the e-mail and Internet system most effectively. They are a preventative measure to minimise the liability of (*company name*).

Computer information systems are defined not only as computers but also as such services as electronic mail (e-mail), the Internet, World Wide Web browsers, word processors, spreadsheets and specific applications, and any other electronic media.

This policy includes the personal use of laptop computers owned and issued by (*company name*) which might be used while employees work at home.

Access

The following factors should be considered:

- Who is entitled to access the Internet?
- How is the e-mail system accessed?
- Are employees entitled to use e-mail for personal use? If so, are there any conditions?
- What about access to other computer areas – in particular, sales/customer databases?

Sample wording

> Access to the Internet has a cost implication, and you will require authorisation from your line manager if you decide your job requires such access.
>
> Access to e-mail must be authorised by the IT manager and a line manager.
>
> Personal use must not be excessive, and must not interfere with the performance of the job. Global e-mails to everyone in the organisation must be authorised and are not allowed for personal use (eg selling items).
>
> Only authorised employees are granted access to the (*company name*) database.

Passwords

The following factors should be considered:

- rules for setting up a password
- rules for changing a password
- warning on disclosing passwords.

Sample wording

> The IT manager will set up a password for you when you first arrive at (*company name*).
>
> You are required to change your password at least once every 45 days.
>
> Your password is confidential and should not be disclosed to any unauthorised person.

Monitoring

Notification should be given that website access may be monitored and that e-mail may be intercepted and read.

Sample wording

(Company name) owns the information systems and has the right to audit them. E-mail messages originating from, received into, or circulating within the *(company name)* e-mail system remain the property of *(company name)* regardless of their physical location. These information systems are monitored on a regular basis, and breaches in the code of conduct may be detected and proven.

If you would like more information about our monitoring systems, and how and why they are carried out, please contact the IT manager.

(Company name) has the right to make information it obtains through this monitoring available internally and/or externally including, where relevant, to such authorities as the police. Personal information held on these systems may be removed without notice. Excessive use of the systems for non-company purposes may result in disciplinary action. Hard copies of inappropriate messages may be used as evidence in disciplinary proceedings.

Time spent on the information systems for recreational use is not routinely monitored and it is therefore the line manager's responsibility to ensure that employees are not abusing this facility. A line manager may prompt an investigation into an individual mailbox.

(*Company name*) reserves the right to inspect any and all files stored in private areas of the network in order to assure compliance with these policies.

Disclaimers

This should specify the wording of the disclaimer and should identify exactly which documents need to have the disclaimer attached to them.

Sample wording

This e-mail contains proprietary information some or all of which may be legally privileged. It is for the intended recipient only. If an addressing or transmission error has misdirected this e-mail, please notify the author by replying to this e-mail. If you are not the intended recipient you must not use, disclose, distribute, copy, print or rely on this e-mail.

When addressed to our clients any opinions or advice contained in this internet e-mail are subject to the terms and conditions expressed in any of (*company name*)'s terms of business. Incoming communications will be monitored.

This e-mail has been swept for computer viruses.

APPENDIX 1

The Internet and World Wide Web

The following items should be included in the policy:

- prohibited access to specified websites
- limitations on browsing the web for non-business purposes
- 'hacking' into another computer or network
- putting material on other sites
- prohibition on downloading or sending offensive material
- explanation of the term 'offensive'
- warnings regarding copyright law
- warnings regarding the use of unchecked information
- those authorised to update or revise the organisation website
- guidelines for dealing with inputs received via the web – which will be different for every organisation.

Sample wording

Employees should not access inappropriate sites, such as those related to pornography, jokes, criminal skills, terrorism, cults, gambling, hate speech, or illegal drugs.

(*Company name*) accepts that staff may find it convenient to browse the Web for their own personal reasons during their own time (eg lunch hour). If you decide to buy anything over the Internet you are advised that, if you give credit card details or other sensitive information, you ensure that you have a secure connection. However, goods cannot be received at work premises.

Employees should not disclose company e-mail addresses. You should not join any mailing lists or solicit any information on the Internet unless there is a pressing need to do so.

It is forbidden to access an external computer or external network without authorisation, or to compromise the performance or privacy of any computer system.

It is forbidden to place any (*company name*) material on any publicly accessible website (including (*company name*)'s own website) unless authorised by the managing director.

You should be aware that those viewing Web pages can be identified by the site owners.

Employees must not access, view, receive, download, send or store material from websites or the Internet:

- *with sexual or pornographic material*
- *related to criminal skills*
- *related to terrorism*
- *related to cults*
- *related to gambling*
- *related to hate speech*
- *related to illegal drugs*
- *that promote or encourage racism or intolerance*
- *that are illegal*
- *that are known to be infected with a virus*

The downloading and/or circulation of such offensive material is considered gross misconduct.

Normal standards of taste and decency apply. The decision as *to whether material breaches this policy is at the discretion of the Managing Director. This list is illustrative, but not exhaustive.*

Employees should take care not to infringe copyright when downloading material or forwarding it to others.

Information received from the Internet should not be used for business purposes until confirmed by a source known to be reliable.

Employees must be authorised to put information onto (*company name*)'s website. Those authorised should ensure that any information posted on the corporate website is accurate and updated regularly.

E-mail

This section of the policy should address the following issues:

- guidelines regarding the disclosure of e-mail addresses
- limitations regarding the private use of e-mail
- wording to be used where e-mail is classified as a 'business letter'
- restrictions on the content/size of the e-mail
- record-keeping, for example complying with VAT requirements to keep records for six years
- avoiding and dealing with misdirected e-mail
- warnings regarding the legal risks, especially defamation
- e-mail etiquette

- understanding when e-mail is an appropriate medium
- warnings regarding viruses.

Sample wording

(*Company name*) reserves the right to retrieve e-mail if it is required for legal evidence.

You should not disclose anyone else's e-mail address without their express permission, nor should you disclose your own unless there is a clear business need.

You may use e-mail for personal matters, but please remember this is a privilege. If you abuse it, disciplinary action may follow. It is also prohibited to send on chain mail.

E-mail should be regarded as any other business communication and treated as a record of the organisation. External e-mail messages should have appropriate signature files, disclaimers and the date attached.

Inappropriate messages are prohibited, including those that are sexually harassing or otherwise offensive to others on the grounds of race, religion, gender, age, disability or appearance. Sending large attachments can effectively halt the e-mail system. If the attachment is larger than 1.5 megabytes it is not suitable for sending via e-mail.

E-mail should not be used for formal communications where permanent records need to be kept. You should ensure that you get confirmation that important external e-mail has been received.

You are advised to take particular care when addressing an e-mail message: it is very easy to select the wrong person from a contacts list or simply to misspell an address. If you receive a misdirected e-mail you should destroy it without reading it and inform the sender.

Employees should not send potentially defamatory e-mail messages that criticise other individuals or organisations or in any way disseminate unsubstantiated rumours. Advice given by e-mail has the same legal bearing as any other written advice. E-mail may create a binding contract and be used as evidence in court hearings.

E-mail messages should not be written in capital letters: this is considered the written equivalent of shouting. E-mail correspondence should be informal and brief, with helpful subject headings (sometimes it is possible to use the subject box for brief messages, thus saving the recipient from having to open the message). Employees are expressly prohibited from sending e-mails that appear to have been sent by someone else (even as a joke).

E-mail should never be used as a medium for disciplining others, or for difficult or sensitive communication (criticising, advising, giving guidance) which is better done on a face-to-face, one-to-one basis.

E-mail may contain viruses or other malicious software. Users should not run or view messages or attachments from unknown senders.

Confidentiality

The policy should also include guidelines regarding the following:

- client-sensitive information
- confidential information
- out-of-office messages.

Sample wording

You are advised not to leave your computer logged on and unattended.

In order to protect our customers we must comply with the Data Protection Act 1998. Customer data must be kept secure, client information on the Internet should be encrypted, and unneeded client information should be carefully disposed of. Owing to the insecure nature of the Internet, no guarantees can be given that an e-mail message has not been read or altered following transmission from *(company name)*.

Highly confidential and valuable information should not be sent by e-mail unless absolutely necessary. Confidential information should not be transmitted by e-mail, unless it is encrypted by a method approved by the IT department. Confidential e-mails should also not be forwarded without the permission of the original sender. Staff should not e-mail items of work to or from home.

If you are absent from the workplace for more than (x) hours/days you should set up an out-of-office message

APPENDIX 1

so that senders of e-mail are aware that you are not at your desk.

General housekeeping

The policy should address the following tasks:

- ensuring in-boxes are not overloaded
- checking e-mail
- loading software.

Sample wording

You should regularly delete old and actioned e-mails. Don't ask for a receipt of your message (unless it is an important external e-mail), and don't send a 'thanks for your message'. Save large attachments onto your hard disk. Remove attachments when responding to e-mail.

You should check your e-mails at the start of the day and at regular (but not too frequent) intervals.

Software must not be loaded onto the system and used without being approved by the IT department and licensed for use. This includes screen savers. Under no circumstances should you use an unapproved browser or install an unapproved patch or plug-in.

Sign off

If at all possible, your employees should give their express consent to these monitoring activities. There are exceptions to the need for it, so careful wording is important here – again, seek legal advice, because the law is changing all the time.

Sample wording

> Failure to comply with these guidelines constitutes a breach of the regulations. Deliberate failure may result in dismissal and may also constitute a criminal offence.
>
> I, (*name*), have read and understood the rules contained within these computer systems policies and agree to the terms of the policies.

Appendix 2: Responsibility for equipment and software

If your organisation has a lot of computer equipment that is specifically allocated to individuals and that is often taken out of the workplace (laptops, for example), it is worthwhile getting that individual to sign for the equipment and confirm his or her responsibility for it. Below is an example of what this form might look like:

JOE BLOGGS
is the authorised (*company name*) guardian of the equipment and software listed below and, as such, may remove it from these premises.

EQUIPMENT DESCRIPTION: ....
SERIAL NUMBER: ....
HARD DISK: ....
RAM: ....
ASSET REF: ....
SOFTWARE: ....

APPROVED:....................(for and behalf of *company name*)
DATE:...................

INTERNET AND E-MAIL USE AND ABUSE

I, Joe Bloggs, accept responsibility for the above equipment and software and take full responsibility for the safe custody of all the above items. I agree to return all of the above items when requested. I also agree to comply with the following guidelines:

- ✓ I will ensure that unauthorised software is not loaded or run on this computer.
- ✓ I will ensure that all disks are checked for viruses before use.
- ✓ I will ensure that the computer is virus-checked regularly.
- ✓ I will ensure that data remains confidential.
- ✓ I will ensure that the computer is not used by any unauthorised person.
- ✓ I will ensure that passwords are used when specified or appropriate.
- ✓ I will treat data that is confidential with great care, ensuring that it is protected and, in particular, not taken anywhere where it could be downloaded or otherwise copied or stolen.
- ✓ I will follow proper back-up procedures.
- ✓ I will ensure the computer is secured or locked away when not in use.

I have read, understood and agreed to *company name*'s computer systems policy.

SIGNED:............................   DATE:............................

Resources

Bibliography and further reading

CENTRAL IT UNIT (CITU) at the Cabinet Office has posted a guide for managers on its website. The guide helps managers balance the individual rights of workers and the need for security and good management. See their website: www.citu.gov.uk

CHARTERED INSTITUTE OF PERSONNEL AND DEVELOPMENT. *The CIPD Training Survey.* London, Chartered Institute of Personnel and Development. Published annually.

CHUTE A., HANCOCK B. *and* THOMPSON M. *The McGraw-Hill Handbook of Distance Learning: A 'how to get started' guide for trainers and human resources professionals.* Maidenhead, McGraw-Hill 1998.

DEPARTMENT OF TRADE AND INDUSTRY. The DTI security-breaches information survey is available from the DTI website, www.dti.gov.uk/cii/bs7799

GONZALEZ J. *The 21st Century Intranet.* New Jersey, Prentice Hall, 1997.

INCOMES DATA SERVICES. *Internet and E-Mail Policies.* IDS Studies 682. London, Incomes Data Services, 2000.

Information Security Breaches Survey 2000, available from the Infosec website, www.infosec.co.uk

INSTITUTE OF MANAGEMENT. *Taking the Strain.* London, Institute of Management, 2000.

KILLIAN C. *Writing for the Web*. Oxford, Self Counsel Press, 1999.

LOGOS. *Internet Recruiting Intelligence Report: Lessons from the Global 500*. July 1999.

RONIN RESEARCH. *Shaming, Blaming and Flaming: Corporate miscommunication in the digital age*. Report commissioned by Novell UK and Ireland and conducted by Ronin Research, 1997.

Organisations

CONTENT TECHNOLOGIES. Sells Minesweeper®, a software for checking e-mails. See www.contenttechnologies.com

DATA PROTECTION REGISTRAR
Wycliffe House
Water Lane
Wilmslow
Cheshire
SK9 5AF
Tel: 01625 545745
Fax: 01625 524510
Website: www.dpr.gov.uk

DELIVERING INFORMATION SOLUTIONS TO CUSTOMERS (DISC)
c:cure Scheme Manager
British Standards Institution
389 Chiswick High Road
London
W4 4AL
Tel: 020 8995 7799
Fax: 020 8996 6411
E-mail: c-cure@bsi.org.uk

There is growing general concern about breaches of information security. The British Standard of information security management (BS7799-1:1999, the Code of Practice for information security management and BS7799-2:1999, the Specification for information security management systems – the criteria for assessment) contains useful guidelines and recommendations for those putting together Internet and e-mail policies. The certificate awarded under BS7799 is called c:cure.

Federation Against Software Theft (FAST)
1 Kingfisher Court
Farnham Road
Slough
Berkshire
SL2 1JF
Tel: 01753 527999
Fax: 01753 532100
E-mail: fast@fast.org
Website: www.fast.org.uk

FAST was founded in 1984 as a not-for-profit organisation supported by the software industry. It provides information and training on issues such as software auditing and security.

Infosecurity: www.infosec.co.uk

Miscellaneous

For information on data protection:
   www.open.gov.uk/dpr/dprhome.htm
For legal advice: www.cyberliability.com

See 'Computeruse' for case studies:
www.incomesdata.co.uk/brief/

WEBSENSE

Websense is a monitoring, reporting and blocking software, costing a minimum of £3 per user: www.websense.com

Recruitment websites

www.antal-int.com
www.bigbluedog.com
www.eotn.co.uk (for small recruiters)
www.futurestep.com (Korn Ferry's site)
www.jobsift.com
www.jobsincharities.co.uk
www.jobsite.co.uk
www.monster.co.uk (world leader)
www.netjobs.co.uk
www.personic.com
www.pp.co.uk
www.recruiter.yahoo.com
www.revolver.co.uk
www.search-direct.com
www.sourceuk.com
www.stepstone.co.uk (European leader)
www.topjobs.net

For others, go to www.rec.uk.com – the website of the UK's Recruitment and Employment Confederation, where another nearly 5,000 recruitment agencies are listed! See also the e-mail address: info@proteusweb.com

Media sites

THE DAILY TELEGRAPH: www.Appointments.plus.com
THE GUARDIAN/THE OBSERVER: www.jobsunlimited.co.uk

Training

ASSOCIATION OF COMPUTER-BASED TRAINING (TACT):
　www.tact.org.uk
CENTRE FOR ADVANCED LEARNING TECHNOLOGIES:
　www.insead.fr/calt/
FORUM FOR TECHNOLOGY IN TRAINING: www.forumtt.org.uk
INSTITUTE FOR COMPUTER-BASED LEARNING (at Heriot-Watt
　University): www.icbl.hw.ac.uk
'Just-in-time' learning: www.learningmatters.com
Learning portal: www.click2learn.com
UNIVERSITY FOR INDUSTRY (UFI): www.ufiltd.co.uk
WEB-BASED TRAINING AND INFORMATION CENTRE: WBTIC is a non-profit resource for those interested in developing and delivering web-based training, online learning or distance education. Here you will find a WBT primer, surveys, discussion forums and resource links: www.filename.com/wbt

Training providers

CLICK2LEARN: www.click2learn.com
DIGITALTHINK: www.digitalthink.com
DISTANCE LEARNING: www.distance-learning.co.uk
LEARNING WORKS: www.mcmillanpartnership.let.uk/
SCOTLAND'S VIRTUAL COLLEGE: www.svc.org.uk
VIRTUAL TRAINING LIBRARY: www.thebiz.co.uk/vtl.asp

Chartered Institute of Personnel and Development

Customer Satisfaction Survey

We would be grateful if you could spend a few minutes answering these questions and return the postcard to CIPD. Please use a black pen to answer. **If you would like to receive a free CIPD pen, please include your name and address.** IPD MEMBER Y/N

....

1. Title of book ....
2. Date of purchase: month .... year ....
3. How did you acquire this book?
   ☐ Bookshop ☐ Mail order ☐ Exhibition ☐ Gift ☐ Bought from Author
4. If ordered by mail, how long did it take to arrive:
   ☐ 1 week ☐ 2 weeks ☐ more than 2 weeks
5. Name of shop .... Town........................ Country ....
6. Please grade the following according to their influence on your purchasing decision with 1 as least influential: (please tick)

	1	2	3	4	5
Title					
Publisher					
Author					
Price					
Subject					
Cover					

7. On a scale of 1 to 5 (with 1 as poor & 5 as excellent) please give your impressions of the book in terms of: (please tick)

	1	2	3	4	5
Cover design					
Paper/print quality					
Good value for money					
General level of service					

8. Did you find the book:
   Covers the subject in sufficient depth ☐ Yes ☐ No
   Useful for your work ☐ Yes ☐ No
9. Are you using this book to help:
   ☐ In your work ☐ Personal study ☐ Both ☐ Other (please state)

Please complete if you are using this as part of a course

10. Name of academic institution..
11. Name of course you are following? ....
12. Did you find this book relevant to the syllabus? ☐ Yes ☐ No ☐ Don't know

Thank you!
To receive regular information about CIPD books and resources call 020 8263 3387.

Any data or information provided to the CIPD for the purposes of membership and other Institute activities will be processed by means of a computer database or otherwise. You may, from time to time, receive business information relevant to your work from the Institute and its other activities. If you do not wish to receive such information please write to the CIPD, giving your full name, address and postcode. The Institute does not make its membership lists available to any outside organisation.

BUSINESS REPLY SERVICE
Licence No WD 1019

Publishing Department
Chartered Institute of Personnel and Development
CIPD House
Camp Road
Wimbledon
London
SW19 4BR